An Insider's Guide to
SURFING

HOPE MERLIN AND NAIMA GREEN

rosen publishing's
rosen central®

NEW YORK

Published in 2015 by The Rosen Publishing Group, Inc.
29 East 21st Street, New York, NY 10010

First Edition

Library of Congress Cataloging-in-Publication Data

Merlin, Hope.
An insider's guide to surfing/Hope Merlin and Naima Green.
  pages cm.—(Sports tips, techniques, and strategies)
Includes bibliographical references and index.
ISBN 978-1-4777-8081-7 (library bound)
ISBN 978-1-4777-8082-4 (pbk.)
ISBN 978-1-4777-8083-1 (6-pack)
1. Surfing—Juvenile literature. I. Green, Naima. II. Title.

GV839.55.M47 2015
797.3'2—dc23

2014020377

Manufactured in Malaysia

Metric Conversion Chart			
1 inch	2.54 centimeters 25.4 millimeters	1 cup	250 milliliters
1 foot	30.48 centimeters	1 ounce	28 grams
1 yard	.914 meters	1 fluid ounce	30 milliliters
1 square foot	.093 square meters	1 teaspoon	5 milliliters
1 square mile	2.59 square kilometers	1 tablespoon	15 milliliters
1 ton	.907 metric tons	1 quart	.946 liters
1 pound	454 grams	355 degrees F	180 degrees C
1 mile	1.609 kilometers		

Contents

CHAPTER 1

Surfing: A History

Captain James Cook was a British explorer, navigator, cartographer, and captain who was the first European to make contact with the eastern coastline of Australia and the Hawaiian Islands, and the first recorded circumnavigator of New Zealand.

In 1778, English sea captain James Cook stood at the bow of his mighty ship, the *Resolution*, while his men surrounded him, looking ahead to their unknown destination. As they sailed toward the islands of Hawaii, Cook's sailors stood in awe, staring at the lush land before them. Steep volcanic cliffs barreled down to the black sand beaches of Kealakekua Bay, the place the Hawaiians call the Pathway of the Gods. As the ship sailed into shallower water, the crew saw brightly colored fish, dashing this way and that throughout the undersea jungle of coral and seaweed. The men saw things they had never imagined. They thought they had found the most beautiful place on Earth.

As they approached the shore, the sailors strained their eyes to catch a glimpse of the native people who gathered along the Hawaiian coast. The men aboard the ship looked to the surrounding ocean for those who might greet them. There were no boats, however, that met Cook's crew in the surf. Instead, it was a Hawaiian kneeling on a long wooden board and gracefully skimming the waves as he approached Cook's ship. This was the first time Europeans had been exposed to this art form that is a complete union of nature and sport, now called surfing.

This 1855 painting by James Gay Sawkins depicts people surfboarding in Hawaii.

When we think of surfing, we often picture a group of tanned young people with brightly colored boards, sliding gracefully near the tips of foamy waves along the coast of untouched white sand beaches. Surfing, however, has very different origins. Surfing was a traditional practice of the indigenous people of Hawaii. Although many of us think of Hawaii as part of the United States, it did not become the fiftieth state until 1959, and was actually an independent nation until 1893. However, the tradition of surfing in Hawaii has remained unchanged through these changes. Surfing has been practiced in the paradise islands of Hawaii for a long time now and has remained an integral part of Hawaiian culture.

Surfing's Birthplace

Around the 4th century, groups of people from the South Pacific islands of Polynesia started traveling the ocean, discovering islands that were previously unknown. Ancient folklore indicates that the islands of Hawaii were discovered by a Polynesian fisherman named Hawai-iloa, who got lost on a long fishing trip. Soon afterward, when other Polynesian travelers heard of the beautiful, untouched islands of Hawaii, many settlers made their way there.

The Polynesians en route to Hawaii were mostly from the small islands of Fiji, Tonga, and Samoa. They were accustomed to traveling thousands of miles in canoes, which were built out of hollowed trees. To shape the canoes, they used objects found in nature, such as stones or bones, as tools.

The original settlers used hollowed trees to build canoes
in which they traveled all the way to Hawaii.

After a boat was constructed came the enormous journey, traveling 2,000 miles across the massive ocean all the way to Hawaii. For navigation, the Polynesians carefully read the clues and signs offered by nature, such as the movement of the wind, the flights of seabirds, and the stars at night. Those who could endure the long trip became the original settlers of the Hawaiian Islands, which historians believe was settled by the 4th century CE.

It is not surprising that a group of people who found their home in Hawaii by traveling the wide ocean would have such a deep connection to it. Not only did the ocean lead them to their new home, but it also sustained the people with its vast natural resources. For islanders such as the Hawaiians, the ocean is the vein that pumps life, food, water, and faith into the heart of the culture. Just as the

Inuit have many words for ice and snow, the people of Hawaii have just as many words for water or ocean. It is even believed that the children of ancient Hawaiians learned how to swim before they learned how to walk!

The ocean, however, was not something the people relied on only for necessities such as travel, nourishment, and religious inspiration. It was also a place the Hawaiians could look to for fun, often in the form of surfing, canoeing, and other water sports.

Surfing was actually a sport practiced by people from all walks of life in ancient Hawaii. Not only did the Hawaiian teenagers practice surfing, Hawaiian royalty did, as well. According to historians, Hawaiian kings and queens would show off their skill and power through surfing! A king or queen was expected to be an extremely skilled surfer. It was extremely embarrassing and their reputations suffered great damage if they had a big wipeout in front of the community.

Certain special boards were only meant to be used by members of royalty. These boards often measured up to twenty-four feet long! The boards used by common people were only about half that length. Hawaiian royalty even had designated beaches where they surfed. If a commoner set foot on that beach, he or she would have to face the consequences of trespassing on royal land.

By the time Captain Cook arrived from Europe, Hawaiians had been settled for generations. It was not until his 1778, trip to the Polynesian Islands, that Cook encountered surfers standing on their boards in Hawaii. He and his crew were captivated—they had never seen something so unique a people riding waves on a piece of wood!

Later, countless other Europeans came to these islands. Many of them were missionaries out to convert the native people to Christianity. After the arrival of the Europeans, however, the surfing culture began declining, mainly because of new restrictions placed on the Hawaiians by the missionaries. For

Created in 1784 by John Webber, a painter aboard Captain Cook's ship, this painting shows the King of Owyhee bringing presents for Captain Cook.

a long time after the Christians arrived in Hawaii, surfing was strictly banned. Surfing would have almost disappeared were it not for a few Hawaiians who surfed in secret, resisting the new rules imposed on them.

By the mid-19th century, Hawaiians began to break away from the strict rules placed on them by the Christian world. They knew that there was nothing negative about surfing. On the contrary, it was an important and enjoyable part of their culture. People started noticing the sport as it reemerged.

"The Duke" of Hawaii

Surfing clubs began popping up all around Hawaiian beaches during the early 1900s, when surfing was still relatively unknown to most Americans. Once the clubs were established, people began to take notice of the sport. Soon, surfing stars were born. One of those budding beach celebrities was named Duke Paoa Kahanamoku, or "the Duke." He was founder of the Hui Nalu Club on the Big Island of Hawaii.

The Duke first became famous as an Olympic champion in freestyle swimming. Then he went on to start his own surf team, market a whole line of surf products, open a nightclub, and even star in Hollywood movies. The Duke was a busy man, and he used his worldwide influence to promote his most beloved pastime—surfing!

The Duke even inspired a classic surfing competition in Hawaii that became legendary during the 1960s and 1970s. To honor the sport's first living legend, this competition, called the Duke Classic, is held annually.

This statue of the Duke stands on the Waikiki beach in Honolulu. The Duke won five gold medals in four Olympic games over a span of twenty-two years.

CHAPTER 2

Surfboard Styles

The best thing about the sport of surfing is that you don't need anything besides your body, a surfboard, and a wave. Also, as a solitary sport, it is possible to practice with just one or two people instead of an entire team. A surfer can decide his or her schedule, influenced only by the waves.

Surfboards today are light and colorful, unlike the heavy wooden ones used earlier.

The History of the Board

It was difficult to handle surfboards back in the days of Captain Cook because they were so heavy. Unlike the light, fiberglass surfboards used today, boards back then were made of hard wood found in the forests. Also, the ancient surfboards were a lot longer, requiring much more strength to haul them through the sand and into the ocean. Plus, when the board got away from a surfer, he or she had a harder time bringing it back into the surf.

At the turn of the 20th century, however, surfboards were being made of different materials—materials that were lighter and stronger than wood found in the Hawaiian forests. Surfboard shapers, the people who make surfboards, began using lighter woods, such as balsa or plywood. These new, lighter boards were much easier to transport through the long stretches of sand that lay before the waves. These boards were also much easier to handle in the ocean.

Beginning in the early 1960s, when surfing's popularity exploded, traditional boards began to change shape radically. Since then, contemporary surfboards have become shorter and shorter. In the late 1960s, the introduction of fiberglass changed the face of surfing. Fiberglass is even lighter and more buoyant than the lightest wood used to make surfboards. Apart from being easier to carry around, it is also easier to perform more advanced maneuvers in the water with fiberglass boards.

Surfboards used to be made of wood. They were much heavier and longer, making them tougher to handle.

11

The Longboard

Longboards, which measured about nine feet or more, were the most common boards before the 1960s. Longboards were the traditional "big guns" of Hawaii. They allowed surfers to ride huge waves, such as those found on the north shore of the Hawaiian island of Oahu.

Surfing changed when shorter boards—around six feet long—hit the scene in the 1960s, and surfers realized how much more mobility they had on them. The boards just kept getting shorter and shorter as surfers realized they could do more stunts and specialty moves with them.

For decades it seemed as though the longboard had vanished from the horizon.

This surfer poses for a photograph with his 11-foot surfboard. These boards, which had been replaced by shorter boards, are now finding a niche market among surfing purists.

However, in recent years, some young surfers brought back the use of the longboard. They started using them as an homage to the ancient Hawaiians, to experience surfing the way it had been before the sport hit the mainstream. These purists attempted surfing with ultralong wooden boards, and with no leashes or special equipment. These longboards allow for much more grace, and sometimes an even longer rides, though it is not possible to perform lots of stunts as longboards are not easily maneuvered.

Longboard Surfing

Your style determines your skill when you're surfing on a longboard. Style is the way the surfer handles the board in the water.

When surfing on a longboard, it is necessary to keep taking small steps to maintain balance.

Since there is more surface area to move around on the longboard, the surfer must take little steps across it during his or her ride. These small, quick steps are to keep the surfer balanced. From the beach, these quick steps look more like a graceful dance. The uniqueness of this "dance," and the elegance with which it is performed, determine the surfer's style. Doing this dance on a short surfboard would be impossible. Some competitions today even have separate categories for the longboard and the shortboard.

Longboards are more difficult to handle than shortboards, especially in steep or quickly rising waves.

Surfboards Today

If you walk into a surf shop today, you would find that you can choose from a large variety of surfboards. You'll need to spend time making your decision and always ask lots of questions. Doing so will ensure that you'll find the right board to meet your needs. Here are the basics on what to look for:

Soft Boards

These foam boards are the lightest yet most durable kind of surfboard. They are also the easiest to handle in the water. Because of their durability, soft boards are the best kind of board for the beginning surfer. They can endure wipeout after wipeout—something the beginner will spend a lot of time doing!

Molded Surfboards

Molded surfboards are made of two sections of fiberglass molded together with a polyurethane (a specific kind of plastic) center. These boards are not as light as the soft boards, yet not as breakable as the custom boards. Molded surfboards are the most popular among surfers with intermediate experience levels.

Custom Boards

Custom boards are another type of light surfboard. As the name implies, these boards can be made specifically for the individual surfer. Surfboard shapers can customize everything about the board, including color, design, and even what kind of wave upon which it should perform best. However, these boards are the most breakable as well as the most expensive. Therefore, it's probably best that these custom boards are left for the expert surfers.

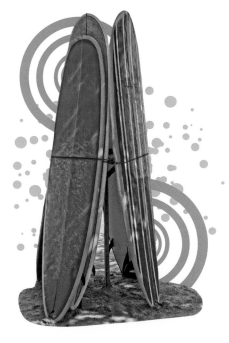

Surfboards are available in many different shapes, colors, and sizes.

The Fin

Some boards have fins, or rudders, attached to the bottom of the board, which give the surfer better control. For years since the dawn of surfing, only one fin was used on the board. However, the development of twin fins during the 1970s was important in the evolution of the surfboard. Twin fins allowed the surfer much more control over his or her board, including helping the surfer gain better mobility when surfing the smaller waves found in shallower waters.

Fins, such as those above, offer better mobility and control to the surfer.

In 1981, surfer Simon Anderson took fin changes even further with the introduction of the triple-fin surfboard. On that first three-fin board, Anderson won the prestigious Bells Beach Contest and became an international surfing celebrity.

Surfboard Accessories

Although the surfer's main tool is his or her board, many choose different accessories to help them along the way. Although these accessories are not always a must, they can make surfing much more comfortable and enjoyable, especially for the novice.

Wax

For better traction, which helps to prevent the surfer from slipping while standing on the board, many

This surfer waxes his board to help him maintain his grip and avoid slipping off.

surfers use surfing wax. Wax is rubbed onto the face, or top side, of the board. Sometimes, sand is applied to the mixture to give the board an even more grippable surface. After all, it would be pretty embarrassing to slip off a board after catching the perfect wave! Before buying wax, be sure to ask an experienced surfer which kind to buy because there are different types for various water temperatures.

Leash

Even though old-time surfers never used this accessory for their surfboards, the invention of the leash has saved many a lost board!

All you need to do is wrap a Velcro strip around your ankle and connect it to your board to make sure that you can retrieve it every time you face a wipeout.

The leash is very useful in retrieving boards that would have otherwise been washed away. Though professional surfers rarely need leashes on their boards, it is best for amateurs to use them as a precautionary measure.

Noseguards

These rubber devices are used to protect the nose, or tip, of some surfboards. This way, scratches and nicks from the ocean floor or coral reefs won't ruin the board. Sometimes, tiny cracks can turn into bigger ones, so this accessory is very handy for prolonging the life of a surfboard.

Wet Suits

Wet suits are body coverings with linings, made so that a surfer can stay in the water for hours without getting cold. Just as marine mammals such as whales and dolphins have an extra layer to protect them from the cold, so should the surfer. Wet suits also protect against scrapes and cuts from the ocean floor. The wet suits for colder and warmer waters are different, which is why it is best to take advice from someone experienced before buying one.

These surfers prefer using wet suits for protection while surfing.

Skim Boards and Boogie Boards: Surfing Without a Surfboard

Shoreline sand at tidal waters is wet from waves coming in and going out. Rounded plywood or fiberglass boards, known as skim boards, are perfect for sliding across these wet sands. This activity is popular with kids, partly because the boards are fairly inexpensive. As the wave is either coming in or going back out to sea (when the depth of the water is only a couple of inches), the skim board is thrown onto the shore and surfed until there is no water left to ride.

This surfer uses a skim board to glide along the shallow waters near the beach.

Boogie boards are foam boards that are much wider than surfboards, but much shorter. Instead of standing up for the ride, the boogie boarder rides waves on his or her belly. That means it takes a lot less energy to ride a great wave! The board performs excellently on small to medium waves, though it could never face the big waves of Oahu's North Shore.

You ride a boogie board on your stomach, which is easier and less tiring than standing and surfing.

CHAPTER 3

Starting to Surf

The first instinct for most beginners is to rush into the water as soon as they reach the beach, but it is important to be patient. It is essential to learn exactly how to approach the surf, and what to do once you're in it. There are some technical moves to learn on the beach before even getting one toe wet. Even though this book will help the beginning surfer learn about the sport, a helpful and patient teacher is highly recommended.

The Popup

Every beginning surfer needs to try his or her hand at the popup maneuver. Starting out crouched in the sand, the novice should try to jump onto his or her board and into the stance of a surfer. "Belly to feet" is another way to describe the popup, and it must be performed in one quick, fluid motion.

This surfer does the popup in the ocean. In a crouching position, she is preparing to stand.

To decide from which side of the board to start, figure out which foot feels best in front. Usually, people tend to know instinctively which way feels natural, but sometimes it is necessary to try the popup on both sides before making a decision. If the left foot is forward, it is in the regular, or most common stance (just like being right-handed). If the right foot is forward, the stance is called goofy-foot. This nickname is not insulting, though to newcomers it may sound that way; it's just how the world of surfing describes putting the right foot in front.

Basically, the beach popup is just practice for what exactly is required in the ocean. Many beginning surfers practice the popup hundreds of times before actually diving in.

Getting Into the Water

Before stepping into the ocean, the surfer first makes sure that all of his or her accessories are being properly held. The surfer must carry the leash in one hand and have it neatly wound around the board for safety. Otherwise, he or she could trip and fall and experience a wipeout before even getting near the water! Also, the board must be carried in a specific way. If there are fins on it, the fins should face in, toward the surfer, who should walk into the ocean with the nose, or tip, facing forward.

Duckdiving

Before actually paddling out to the big waves, it is important to try out more maneuvers in order to be completely prepared. Sometimes it is best to try out these moves in shallow water first.

A duckdive in action.

As the surfer paddles out into deeper water, he or she comes upon white water, the foamy area of the surf created after a wave crashes. To bypass the white water without getting toppled over, it is necessary to learn a move called the duckdive.

Ducking your head under the waves that are about to crash into you is called duckdiving. The impact from oncoming waves is reduced this way.

A successful duckdive resembles the movements of a duck or seabird looking for food underwater. Usually with one knee propped on the board, the surfer dunks his or her head under the water just behind the front of the board, with his or her head tucked under the neck area, like a duck. Once under the water, the board's buoyancy causes the board

This surfer prepares to duckdive. He crouches on the board and gets ready to dunk his head under the water.

to shoot up toward the surface again, safely past the waves. Until he or she paddles out past the white water, the surfer continues doing this maneuver.

In the deeper waters, surfers wait for their turn in a line.

The Lineup

The surfer can now look for the "lineup" once he is well past the white water and has plenty of practice on both the beach and smaller waves.

As the surfer paddles out into deeper and deeper water, he or she will notice a line of other surfers, all waiting for the perfect wave. Just as in everyday life, when waiting in line it is considered rude to jump in front of the person ahead of you. The same rule of thumb applies in surfing. The beginning surfer may learn the hard way if he or she attempts skipping another surfer in the lineup. What would happen if you jumped in front of the line at a grocery store?

Once in the lineup, the surfer must look for many things in order to catch the perfect wave. The best way to achieve this sense is by watching other surfers and paying attention to the kinds of waves that they ride. Watch for the waves that create successful rides, and for the waves that wipe out surfers. As is the case with all other sports, time, patience, and the willingness to ask for advice when in doubt is required to learn how to surf.

Riding the Perfect Wave

All surfers should try to catch the wave just as it is beginning to break. At the same time, he or she should try to steady him or herself on the board and attempt a popup, just like beginners practice on the beach. In one quick motion, the surfer should move smoothly from the water to the board, or belly to board. Many beginners get discouraged after their first attempts at standing on the board, but it is necessary to try again and again. It sometimes takes beginners several practice waves before being able to stand successfully on a moving board.

When preparing for a day of surfing, the novice should always follow the clues he or she receives from nature to determine the surf. It is important to remember that the best surfers see the ocean as something they must combine themselves with, not fight against. It takes perfect harmony of both ocean and surfer to achieve the best ride possible.

The best surfers hit the beach really early, sometimes before the sun even rises. These early hours are said to have the most optimum conditions as the waves are at their highest because of early-morning high tides. Take it from the pros and go out early!

Mastering small waves in shallow waters before venturing out into the deeper portions is very important.

Surfing Manners

The beginning surfer must be aware of a few rules of etiquette, including being respectful to other surfers when successfully navigating the waves. These rules also help the surfer gain respect in the lineup and make friends.

This surfer enjoys riding the wave on his belly
before attempting to stand up.

Surfing and Sharks

There are few words in the English language that evoke as much fear in a surfer as "shark." Sharks are among the most feared creatures in the ocean, and possibly in the world. Some spiritual surfers see the shark as their protector, but many contemporary surfers see sharks as their strongest adversaries in the ocean.

This surfer is unaware of the danger that lurks beneath the surface of the water. Fortunately, shark attacks are not as common as they are made out to be.

Different nicknames exist for different sharks, depending on a surfer's geographic location. For instance, in Australia, the shark most commonly linked to shark attacks is the infamous great white, or the "man in the grey suit." In tropical areas where the water is warm, tiger sharks, or "terries," are mainly responsible for shark attacks. However, shark attacks are extremely rare.

The most important thing to remember is that humans are not part of a shark's natural diet. If a shark attacks, it is only because the shark thinks that the surfer or swimmer is a seal, an otter, or another marine mammal. Like any wild animal, the shark is quite possibly more afraid of you than you are of it. Before going surfing for the first time, consider doing a bit of research on sharks. Find out which ones pose the most threat in your surfing area and follow advice on how to avoid attracting them.

The Right of Way

One of the most important rules in surfing is the right of way, just as it is in driving. The first surfer on a particular wave, or the surfer who is closest to the curl of the wave, has the right of way. The curl is the part of the wave that creates a tunnel when it is just about to break. This basically means that if someone is already riding a wave, get out of the way.

The surfer closest to the curl of the wave gets the right to ride the wave. Other surfers scramble to move out of the way.

Help Other Surfers in Distress

Accidents do happen. If you see one but cannot paddle out to help a surfer in distress, be sure to call out to other surfers in the surrounding area. This rule is one of the most important ones in surfing. Everyone should be willing to sacrifice even the most perfect wave if a fellow surfer requires help.

Hold Your Board

Don't ever let go of your surfboard, especially around crowds or in the presence of other surfers. A runaway board could hurt someone, plus, you may lose your precious surfboard.

Avoid Fights

The lineup can be a very competitive place, and new surfers may well be picked on a little. If any surfer seems overly aggressive, just avoid him or her. It is not a good idea to fight or argue, especially over a wave.

Don't Surf Waves You Can't Handle

You may find yourself at the mercy of the overwhelmingly powerful waves of the ocean. Know your limitations. In other words, a beginning surfer shouldn't expect to paddle out and ride the biggest wave around. It's a good idea to leave the big waves to the pros, or you might end up getting hurt.

This surfer is experienced enough to handle and manage a wave as huge as this one.

It's best if amateur surfers such as these stick to smaller waves in shallow waters.

This rule also helps with overcrowding, as it instructs the inexperienced surfer to free up lineup space for waves he or she cannot yet surf.

Don't "Drop In"

Never dropping in on another surfer means never charging a wave that someone else is already riding. Dropping in can lead to collisions between surfers and cause serious injuries. "Snaking" someone is just as bad. Dropping in usually differs from snaking in one way: snakers come in from the side and whip in front of another surfer whereas in dropping in, the surfer "steals" the wave from behind.

Importance of Safety

Sometimes it is easy to become carried away by the excitement and beauty of the ocean and the surf. But it is important to understand that safety comes first. Do not take any unnecessary risks. Wait until you are an experienced and well-traveled surfer before attempting the big waves.

Never Surf Alone

Though you may want to experience the tranquility of the ocean at first light alone, it is always safer to take along a friend. The ocean is powerful and unpredictable. You could drown, you could run into trouble with dangerous sea animals, or you could get caught up in a reef too deeply. A friend should be surfing with you at all times to help you out in case of an emergency—and vice versa.

Surfing alone, especially for beginners, is very dangerous.

It's always safer to surf in a large group.

Before Paddling Out, Watch the Ocean for at Least Thirty Minutes

When paddling out to the lineup, pay close attention to the face of the ocean. Look for abnormalities on the surface, which might indicate the presence of rocks, reefs, or shallow water.

Remember to Wear Sunscreen

Exposure to the sun can be dangerous, especially since the sun's rays are actually magnified by the surface of the water. Always wear a waterproof sunscreen with an SPF of at least 30 when surfing.

Be Aware of Currents or Riptides

Strong, pounding waves are not the only thing to watch out for in the ocean. Riptides are strong currents in the ocean that can pull a surfer or swimmer out to sea. When caught in a riptide, it is advisable to swim or paddle parallel to the shore until the current subsides, and then swim back to the shore. Do not swim straight back toward the beach and do not swim directly against the current. Swim in the direction that offers the least resistance.

Surfing Lingo

The world of surfing has its own lingo (slang) of sorts. If the beginning surfer studies up on these words and phrases, he or she might make an impression in the lineup!

Bone crusher: A big wave that breaks with extreme force.

Buoy: Someone who floats around, never takes a wave, and is often in the way.

Carving up the mob: Australian term for a reckless ride as one surfer cuts through a group of surfers or swimmers.

This wave is quite a bone crusher!

Casper: A nickname for a tourist or newcomer who has yet to get a tan— named after the famous friendly cartoon ghost.

Stickbug stance: Riding a longboard, squatting with your feet spread wide apart and your backside sticking out.

This surfer is in a stickbug stance.

Tubular: Cool or excellent, as in "totally tubular."

Walking the dog: Altering speed by walking forward and backward on a surfboard.

CHAPTER 4

Getting Involved

Surfing isn't the same as it was when Captain Cook first arrived in Hawaii. Ever since surfing had its renaissance, or "new beginning," in the 1960s, it has become a sport that has attracted much attention from advertisers and sponsors worldwide. By the late 1970s, surfing contests had begun popping up all over the world. They were not restricted to Hawaii, California, and Australia, but rapidly spread to South Africa, Japan, and Brazil. Large international sponsors such as Coca-Cola are willing to give huge money prizes to the best of the best in the ocean. For those who have risen to the top, surfing can be a very lucrative pastime.

Floridian Kelly Slater is considered by many to be the best surfer of all time. Here, he is photographed at the 2010 Men's Rip Curl Pro in Portugal.

Professional Surfing

In 1977, surfing promoter Fred Hemmings Jr., organized a worldwide surf tour for professionals. It took place in thirteen separate contests across the globe. The tour was a resounding success and pro surfing was here to stay.

Although the contests helped the sport gain international interest with coverage on radio and television, there were flaws in the system. Thanks to changing wave conditions, surfers in competitions sometimes had completely different surf experiences. Different maneuvers were possible in different waves, which affected points and scoring. One surfer might be lucky enough to catch the perfect wave while another equally talented surfer might never catch a decent wave. Since the contests were judged mainly on these maneuvers, the result was a dilemma in scoring.

Another problem with such contests was how one entered the event. Getting into a competition was nearly impossible unless you knew someone important such as another pro surfer or a competition judge. A fair way to enter surfers' competitions became extremely important for contest organizers. Because surfing is traditionally such an exclusive sport (getting onto any great surf spot is very difficult for a newcomer), it was difficult for rookies to break into the pro circuit.

Californian Pat Gudauskas and Kelly Slater compete during the Quicksilver Pro Surf Cup on March 3, 2011, in Snappers Rocks, NSW, Australia.

To solve this problem, events such as the Pro Class Trials were created. In these events, unknown surfers from across the globe have a fair chance at entering the contests. Today there are several huge surfing competitions that use trials to admit new, unknown surfers. These competitions occur worldwide throughout the year. After all, when it's winter in North America, the waves are just perfect in Australia!

Scoring at a Surfing Competition

The criteria has changed significantly over the years in terms of scoring in a surfing competition. Traditionally, one whole ride was scored by a judge. Now, each special move or maneuver is judged with a specific amount of points awarded. The surfer receives points during his or her allotted time in the waves (often fifteen minutes in length), which are added together for his or her score.

Usually, the competitions are arranged in heats, or short trials, in which the surfers have a chance to prove their stuff. These heats can last anywhere from five minutes to fifteen minutes, sometimes even longer. In some heats, four surfers compete at the same time. Most competitions have both individual and team events.

Hawaiian Granger Larsen surfs a big wave at the Men's Open championship in the Honolua Legends of the Bay Surf contest at Honolua Bay, January 20, 2013.

All competitions have slightly different rules, but for the most part, competition scoring has four parts: Radically Controlled Maneuvers, Most Critical Section, the Biggest and/or Best Waves, and Longest Functional Distance. These criteria are decided by the International Surfing Association (ISA), the organization that oversees most contests worldwide. Different regions and competitions run by smaller organizations may have different rules and scoring.

The Endless Summer

In 1966, filmmaker/surfer Bruce Brown, taking advantage of the buzz about surfing in California, made a classic documentary, *The Endless Summer*. The film charted the adventures of American surfers Robert August and Mike Hynson as they searched the globe for "the perfect wave." Their travels led them to places where few, if any, had surfed before:—Africa, Australia, and even parts of South America. The movie was a huge hit, especially among the surfing culture.

A poster for the 1966 film, *The Endless Summer,* is seen here.

Shown above is a slab in the Surfer's Hall of Fame in honor of Bruce Brown.

In 2002, Brown's son Dana made another surfing movie, *Step into Liquid*, in his father's tradition. Learning and appreciating this amazing sport is now much easier, thanks to the Browns and other surfing filmmakers.

Surfing Superstars

Over the ages, there have been many surfing superstars. Today, three surfers are acknowledged as the active legends of the sport—Kelly Slater, Sunny Garcia, and Rob Machado.

One of the world's most talented surfers, Kelly Slater (born February 11, 1972, Florida) won his first world title at age 20 and his 11th at age 39, making him the oldest and youngest surfer to have won the Association of Surfing Professionals (ASP) championship.

Sunny Garcia won the Association of Surfing Professionals World Tour Champion (ASP WCT) in 2000. As of 2014, he holds the record for the most World Qualifying Series (WQQS) wins.

Rob Machado has a very casual, laid back style, both in the water and out of it.

Slater has graced the cover of many surfing magazines and has a full line of endorsements. Some call him the best surfer of all time. Aside from the near million dollars he has earned in contest money, he has brought home more than twice that amount in endorsements. These accomplishments, along with the skill and determination required to be the best athlete in any sport, make him an international surfing superstar.

Hawaiian Sunny Garcia (born January 14, 1970, Hawaii) has remained on the list of international surfing's top sixteen players since 2004. Garcia is one of the most recognizable surfing stars. He has been competing on the international circuit for more than seventeen years and to date has earned more than $1 million in winnings in his career.

Sydney-born Rob Machado (born October 16, 1973, Sydney) is one of the most famous goofyfoot surfers of all time. At the age of 11, Machado began surfing while living in San Diego, California, where his family had moved. He is in the top league of surfers and has won almost every existing contest.

Women Surfers

Women surfers date all the way back to ancient Hawaii. Since surfing regained popularity in the 20th century, women have participated in the sport, as well. In fact, when Duke Paoa Kahanamoku visited Australia with his surfboard in 1915, a woman rode with him. Her name was Isabel Letham, and she was the first Australian ever to surf!

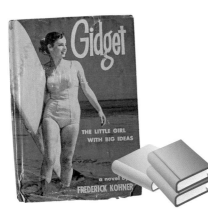

Gidget first appeared in a book written by Frederick Kohner in 1957.

Just as women in politics, business, and other professions have struggled to receive recognition for their achievements, so have women in the world of surfing. The pioneers of women's surfing provided the inspiration for the younger generations of women to come. Television and the movies also played a role in opening the door for women surfers. During the 1960s, Gidget was a popular character in several movies and a television series. Gidget was a teenager who spent her summers surfing in Malibu, California. The popularity of this character inspired many young women to try surfing. Soon enough, there were many women joining the lineup, riding the waves right alongside the men.

Women who surf sometimes have a different mentality than their male counterparts. U.S. female surfing pioneers Rell Sunn and Jericho Poppler commented in *The History of Surfing*: "Boys are out there to prove they can conquer the waves … but girls are more like artists who work their choreography and go out to dance routines set up by the situation the waves dictate."

Portuguese surfer Joana Rocha is photographed here at the Nazare Surf Pro in Portugal, 2010.

Born in Pennsylvania and raised in California, Margo Oberg (born September 8, 1953) was the most respected and recognizable woman surfer in the 1960s. She competed well into the 1970s and won the Bells Beach women's division in Australia. Following Oberg's lead, in the 1980s Australian Pam Burridge dazzled the surfing world with her talented board work. From the late 1980s to 2002, when she retired from competition, American Lisa Anderson, collected dozens of trophies in the contest circuit. Anderson remains a role model for aspiring women surfers. And their love for surfing has never stopped.

Surfing and Modern Technology

For those aspiring surfers who live near the coastline, there are always plenty of waves. Seaside towns, especially those known for having great surfing spots, are perfect places for kids to get a year-round education in surfing. But for kids who are landlocked, living nowhere near the ocean, there are alternatives.

Wave Pools

Wave pools give people all over the world, regardless of their geographic location, the opportunity to try surfing. Through the use of high-powered pumps and reservoirs, wave pools simulate the ocean. Today, the machinery in wave pools has evolved to include different types of waves, including half pipes and easy peaks.

Wave pools such as this one help people all over the world enjoy the sport of surfing, regardless of their location.

Tow-Ins

In the 1970s, tow-ins gained popularity. Surfers had always known that the biggest waves sometimes crash miles from the coast on outer reefs—far out of reach from the paddling surfer. In the 20th century, the creation of wave such as jet skis made reaching the biggest waves possible. Large boats and even helicopters are sometimes used to assist the surfer in making it to the outer reefs.

Large waves are found far out in the ocean
and are inaccessible to the average surfer.

After being towed in, the surfer generally uses a special board—one fitted with straps to keep the surfer safely atop and attached securely to the board. Although some surfers use smaller boards (seven feet two inches and up), the bulk of tow-in surfers prefer the big guns (nine feet six inches and up), mainly because of the power they provide. Tow-in surfing is extremely dangerous, and only surfing daredevils will even attempt it. They describe the experience as completely unique—something they will do for the rest of their lives.

Surfing Spin-Offs

Since the popularity of surfing exploded in the 1960s, manufacturers have tried to devise spin-off surfing activities. The market expanded and surfers' specific needs were targeted.

Skateboarding

Skateboarding is, undoubtedly, surfing's most popular spin-off. Introduced in 1963, skateboarding became a national craze almost overnight. Before long,

however, kids started losing interest, and by the mid-1960s, the skateboard had all but disappeared.

Then a team of bad-boy surfers from an area of a Southern California beach nicknamed "Dogtown" turned to skateboarding after the fleeting morning waves had subsided for the day. During surfing downtime, these kids—called the Zephyr Skate Team—practiced their surfing moves on skateboards day in and day out. When they saw famous surfer

Skateboarding, a popular spin-off of surfing, is now a major sport in itself.

Larry Bertlemann do a cutback for the first time, they decided to attempt it on a skateboard. Thus, modern-day skateboarding was born all because a few bored surfers couldn't catch their waves!

Windsurfing

In the 1930s, U.S. surfer Tom Blake began toying with attaching sails to his surfboard. It wasn't until the 1980s, however, that windsurfing became a popular sport. The benefits of surfing with a sail were obvious: no paddling, few crowds, and very high speeds. The windsurfer can also ride all different kinds of waves. Less effort is also required, as the surfer is propelled by the force of the wind.

Windsurfing is another spin-off of surfing that has gained popularity.

Snowboarding

The combination of surfing and skiing gave rise to a new sport:— snowboarding. Instead of wearing two skis, the participant is firmly strapped to a surfboard-like board. With this innovation, it is possible to surf mountaintops covered in snow! In other words, the snowboard basically surfs waves of snow. Developed in the 1960s, many ski resorts have come to include half pipes on their slopes for hot dogging snowboarders.

Snowboarding is an added tourist attraction for many mountainous regions.

Getting Involved

There are many ways to get started and learn about surfing, even if you don't live near a beach. There are numerous websites where you can learn about contests and surfing celebrities, surfing equipment, competition rules, and so on. There are even chat rooms for young surfers such as yourself, just wanting to learn more about the sport.

The Hawaiians knew it, and now the world does, too—there's nothing like surfing! Since this ancient pastime has taken the form of a contemporary craze, the world cannot get enough of it. Not only is it fun, but talented surfers can even make careers out of their favorite pastime.

One of the things that will keep the wannabe surfer coming back for more is the simplicity of the sport. With just a body and a board, surfers have discovered that it is possible to become one with nature, simply by riding its billowing waves, having fun, and being stoked.

Time shows that surfing is here to stay. As long as there are waves to catch, there will be amateurs and surf stars alike to go ride them.

Glossary

buoyant Having the ability to float.

bypass To pass by going around.

cutback Making a powerful turn back toward the breaking part of a wave.

decline To become smaller in number.

evoke To call forth or bring out.

fiberglass A material made of glass and plastics.

heat A round in a race or competition.

influence A person, event or situation that affects something in an important way.

instinctive Done on impulse; spontaneous and unthinking.

integral Necessary to make something complete.

lingo The special language of a particular field of interest.

lucrative Producing wealth.

maneuver An intended and controlled movement.

missionary A person sent to a foreign country to carry on an activity, especially religious.

mobility The ability to move from one place to another.

novice A person new to a field or activity; a beginner.

reservoirs Bodies of stored water.

resist To remain firm against the pressure.

stocked Enthusiastic.

wipeout A sudden fall off a surfboard.

For More Information

Eastern Surfing Association
P.O. Box 582
Ocean City, MD 21843
(866) 787-3372
Website: http://www.surfesa.org/home

International Surfing Association
5580 La Jolla Blvd. PMB 145
La Jolla, CA 92037
(858) 551-5292
Website: http://www.isasurf.org/

International Surfing Museum
P.O. Box 782
Huntington Beach, CA 92648
(714) 960-3483
Website: http://www.surfingmuseum.org

Websites

Because of the changing nature of Internet links, Rosen Publishing, has developed an online list of websites related to the subject of this book. This site is updated regularly. Please use this link to access the list:

http://www.rosenlinks.com/STTS/Surf

For Further Reading

Almond, Elliot. *Surfing: Mastering Waves from Basic to Intermediate (Mountaineers Outdoor Expert)*. Seattle, WA: Mountaineers Books, 2009.

Burkard, Chris. *Distant Shores: Surfing The Ends Of The Earth*. AMMO Books, Pasadena, CA, 2010.

Hamilton, Laird. *Force of Nature: Mind, Body, Soul, And, of Course, Surfing*. New York, NY: Rodale Books, 2010.

Heller, Peter. *Kook: What Surfing Taught Me About Love, Life, and Catching the Perfect Wave*. New York, NY: Free Press, 2010.

Kempton, Jim. *Surfing: The Manual: Advanced*. Hawaii: Hedonist Surf Co., 2008.

Olsen, Richard. *A Golden Age: Surfing's Revolutionary 1960s and '70s*. New York, NY: Rizzoli, 2013.

Robison, John. *Surfing Illustrated: A Visual Guide to Wave Riding*. Blacklick, OH: International Marine/Ragged Mountain Press, 2010.

Warshaw, Matt. *The History of Surfing*. San Francisco, CA: Chronicle Books, 2010.

Westwick, Peter. *The World in the Curl: An Unconventional History of Surfing*. New York, NY: Random House, 2013.

Yogis, Jaimal. *Saltwater Buddha: A Surfer's Quest to Find Zen on the Sea*. Somerville, MA: Wisdom Publications, 2009.

Bibliography

Bizley, Kirk. *Surfing*. Chicago: Heinemann Library Press, 2000.

Cralle, Trevor. *The Surfin'ary: A Dictionary of Surfing Terms and Surf Speak*. Berkeley, CA: Ten Speed Press, 2001.

Hemmings, Fred. *The Soul of Surfing*. New York: Thunder's Mouth Press, 1997.

Maclaren, James. *Learn to Surf*. New York: Lyons and Burford, 1997.

Turner, Stephen. *Windsurfing*. New York: Gallery Books, 1986.

Young, Nat, with Craig McGregor. *The History of Surfing*. Tucson, AZ: Body Press, 1987.

Index

Index

About the Authors

Florida-born writer Hope Merlin, while not a surfer herself, has long been an admirer and follower of the sport. Merlin lives in New York City, where her pastimes include recreational soccer and Ultimate Frisbee.

Naima Green is a professional surfer who travels all around the world, competing in different surfing competitions. When she is not surfing, she works as a writer in New York City.

Photo Credits